AI WORLD
AI IN MEDICINE

by Ford Chambers

pogo

Ideas for Parents and Teachers

Pogo Books let children practice reading informational text while introducing them to nonfiction features such as headings, labels, sidebars, maps, and diagrams, as well as a table of contents, glossary, and index.

Carefully leveled text with a strong photo match offers early fluent readers the support they need to succeed.

Before Reading

- "Walk" through the book and point out the various nonfiction features. Ask the student what purpose each feature serves.
- Look at the glossary together. Read and discuss the words.

Read the Book

- Have the child read the book independently.
- Invite them to list questions that arise from reading.

After Reading

- Discuss the child's questions. Talk about how they might find answers to those questions.
- Prompt the child to think more. Ask: Would you want a robot doctor? Why or why not?

Pogo Books are published by Jump!
5357 Penn Avenue South
Minneapolis, MN 55419
www.jumplibrary.com

Copyright © 2025 Jump!
International copyright reserved in all countries. No part of this book may be reproduced in any form without written permission from the publisher.

Library of Congress Cataloging-in-Publication Data

Names: Chambers, Ford, author.
Title: AI in medicine / by Ford Chambers.
Description: Minneapolis, MN: Jump!, Inc., [2025]
Series: AI world | Includes index.
Audience: Ages 7–10
Identifiers: LCCN 2024025995 (print)
LCCN 2024025996 (ebook)
ISBN 9798892135658 (hardcover)
ISBN 9798892135665 (paperback)
ISBN 9798892135672 (ebook)
Subjects: LCSH: Artificial intelligence—Medical applications—Juvenile literature.
Classification: LCC R859.7.A78 M324 2025 (print)
LCC R859.7.A78 (ebook)
DDC 610.285—dc23/eng/20240701
LC record available at https://lccn.loc.gov/2024025995

Editor: Alyssa Sorenson
Designer: Emma Almgren-Bersie

Photo Credits: Shutterstock, cover (machine); Trifonov_Evgeniy/iStock, cover (screen); hxdbzxy/Shutterstock, 1; Ken Weinrich/Shutterstock, 3; Ociacia/Shutterstock, 4; VesnaArt/Shutterstock, 5; FatCamera/iStock, 6; Moment Makers Group/iStock, 7; AnnaStills/iStock, 8–9; Moyo Studio/iStock, 10–11; Dragos Condrea/iStock, 12–13; Morsa Images/iStock, 14–15; Eakkapon Sriharun/Shutterstock, 16 (computer); Adisak Riwkratok/Shutterstock, 16 (screen); Zoran Zeremski/iStock, 17; amenic181/Shutterstock, 18–19; Gorodenkoff/Shutterstock, 20–21; Studio Romantic/Shutterstock, 21; Africa Studio/Shutterstock, 23.

Printed in the United States of America at Corporate Graphics in North Mankato, Minnesota.

TABLE OF CONTENTS

CHAPTER 1
What Is AI? 4

CHAPTER 2
Smart Medicine 6

CHAPTER 3
Medicine of the Future 16

ACTIVITIES & TOOLS
Try This! 22
Glossary 23
Index 24
To Learn More 24

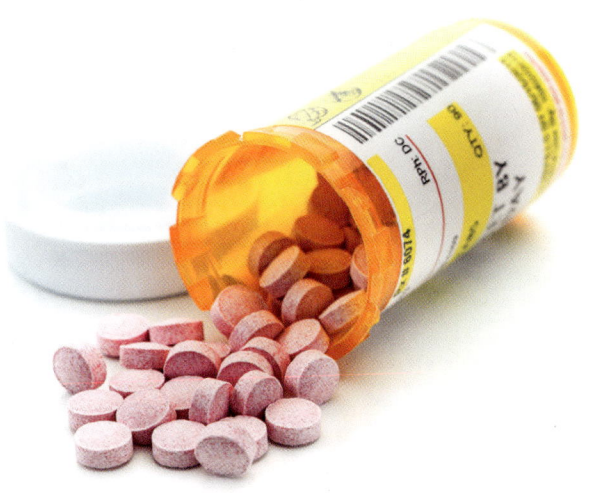

CHAPTER 1
WHAT IS AI?

Imagine you are sick. You go to the doctor. Instead of a human doctor, a **robot** sees you! It asks how you feel. The robot **swabs** your nose to test what you are sick with.

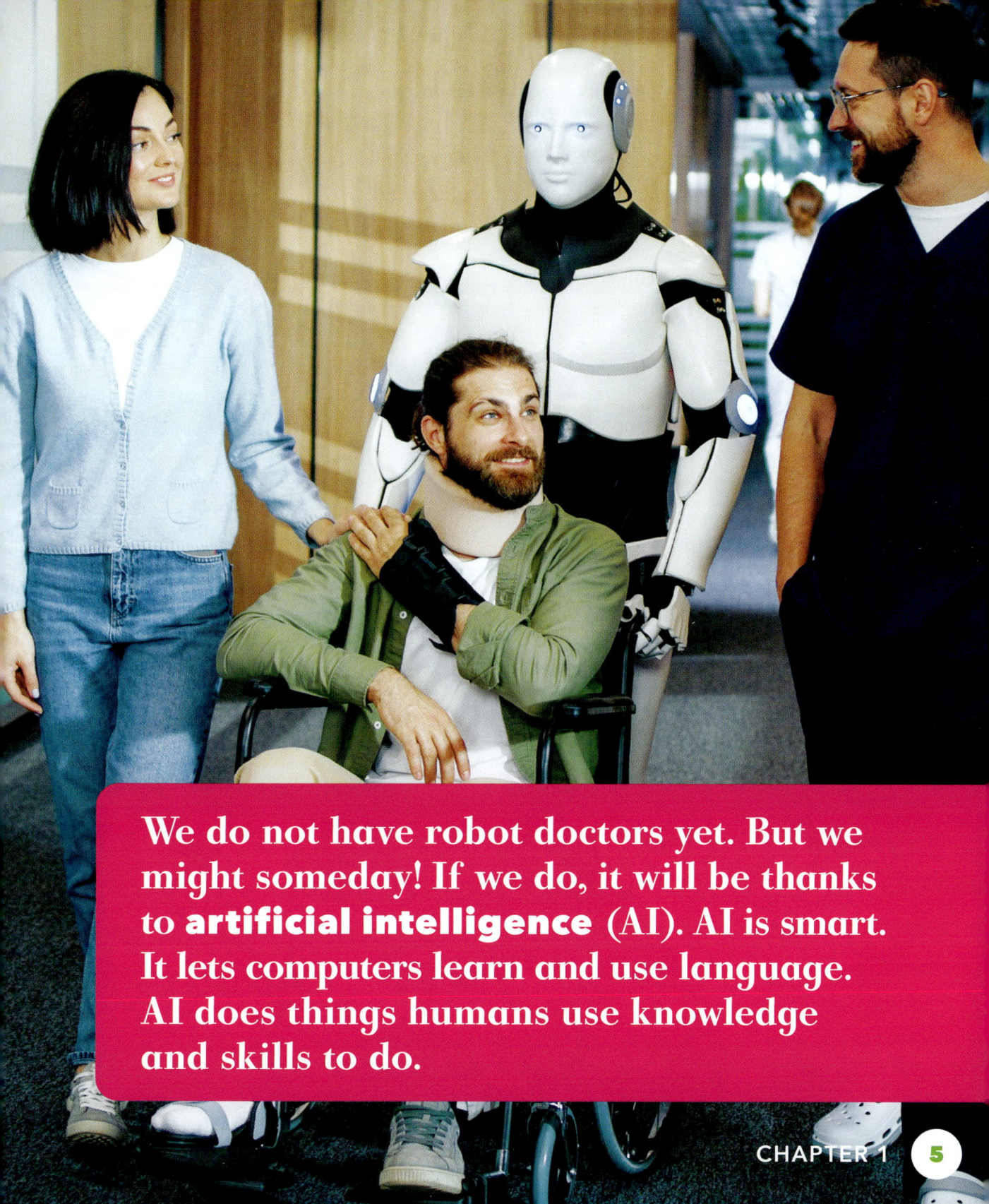

We do not have robot doctors yet. But we might someday! If we do, it will be thanks to **artificial intelligence** (AI). AI is smart. It lets computers learn and use language. AI does things humans use knowledge and skills to do.

CHAPTER 1

CHAPTER 2
SMART MEDICINE

AI helps doctors care for **patients**. Doctors take notes. They write down how you are feeling.

This information goes in your record. This shows your health history. It has test results. It lists **medicines** you take.

AI makes it easier for doctors to take notes. How? A doctor talks to a patient about their **symptoms**. A computer with AI listens. AI makes a **summary** of the conversation. The doctor doesn't have to type the notes. They have time to see more patients!

> **DID YOU KNOW?**
>
> AI can miss important things. It can even make things up. People should check AI summaries to make sure they are correct.

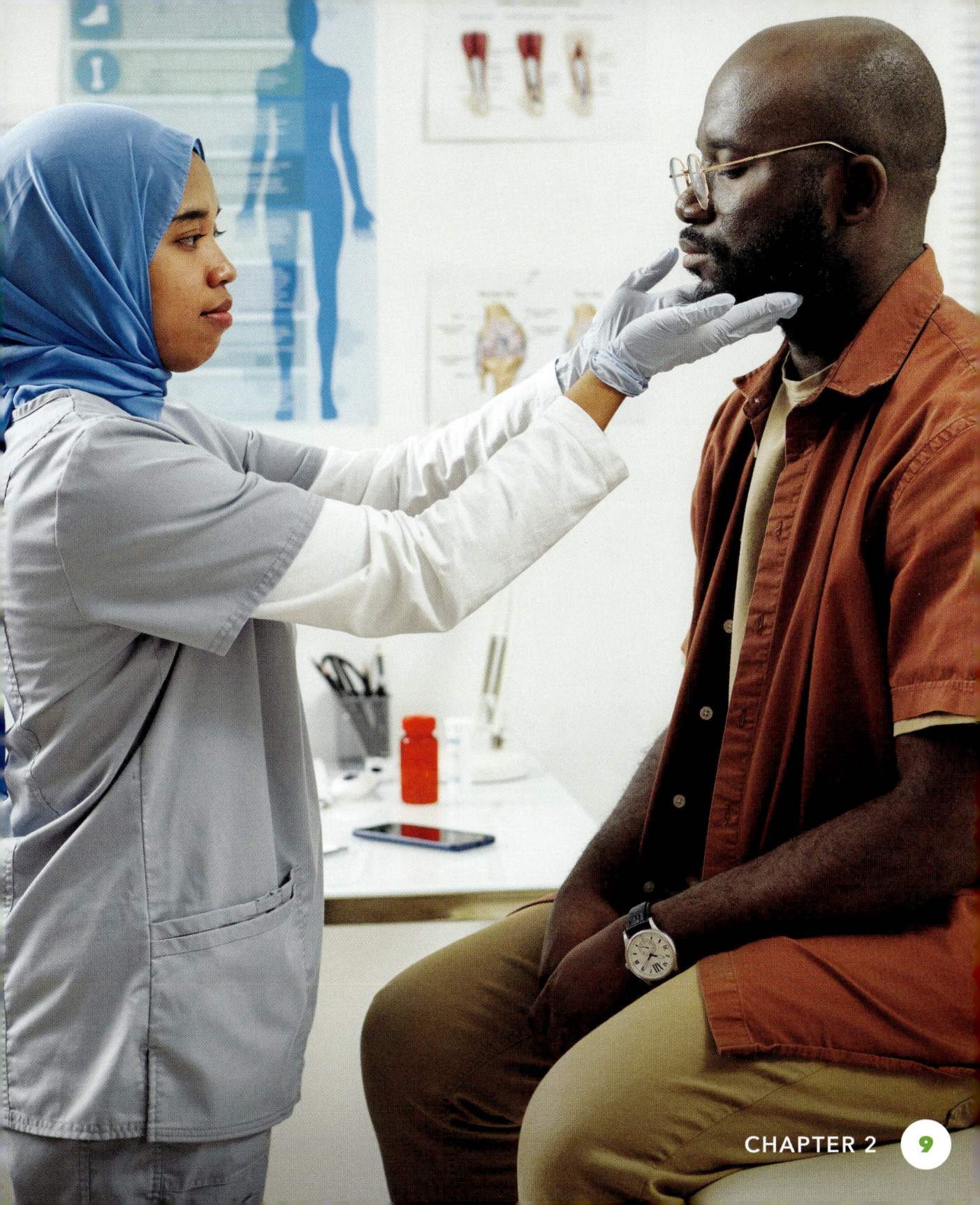

CHAPTER 2

AI **chatbots** also help. They message patients. They ask questions. They answer some, too. Is a patient still sick? The chatbot tells the doctor. The doctor calls the patient.

TAKE A LOOK!

How does a chatbot conversation work? Take a look!

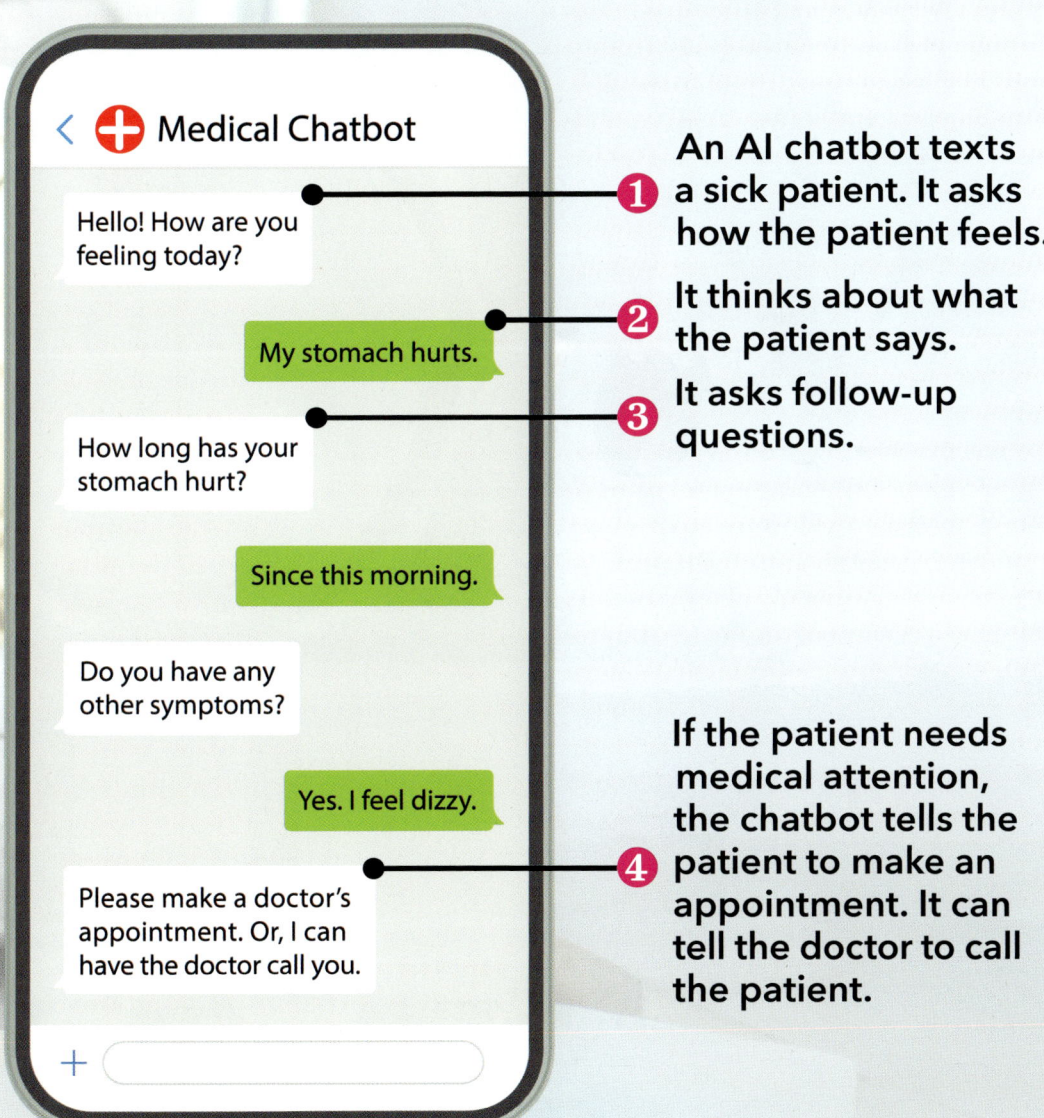

1. An AI chatbot texts a sick patient. It asks how the patient feels.
2. It thinks about what the patient says.
3. It asks follow-up questions.
4. If the patient needs medical attention, the chatbot tells the patient to make an appointment. It can tell the doctor to call the patient.

AI can help **diagnose**, too. An AI program has been trained to spot signs of **cancer**. It looks at **MRI** images. It tells doctors what it sees.

DID YOU KNOW?

In 1986, DXplain was created. It is a computer program. It is still used today. It helps doctors. How? A doctor gives it a patient's symptoms. DXplain uses AI to suggest possible illnesses.

CHAPTER 2   13

AI also helps make new medicines. How? Many medicines are made with chemicals. AI learns about them. It comes up with new chemical recipes. Scientists test them!

CHAPTER 2

CHAPTER 3

MEDICINE OF THE FUTURE

AI is getting smarter. AI in medicine will only get better. It will help more people.

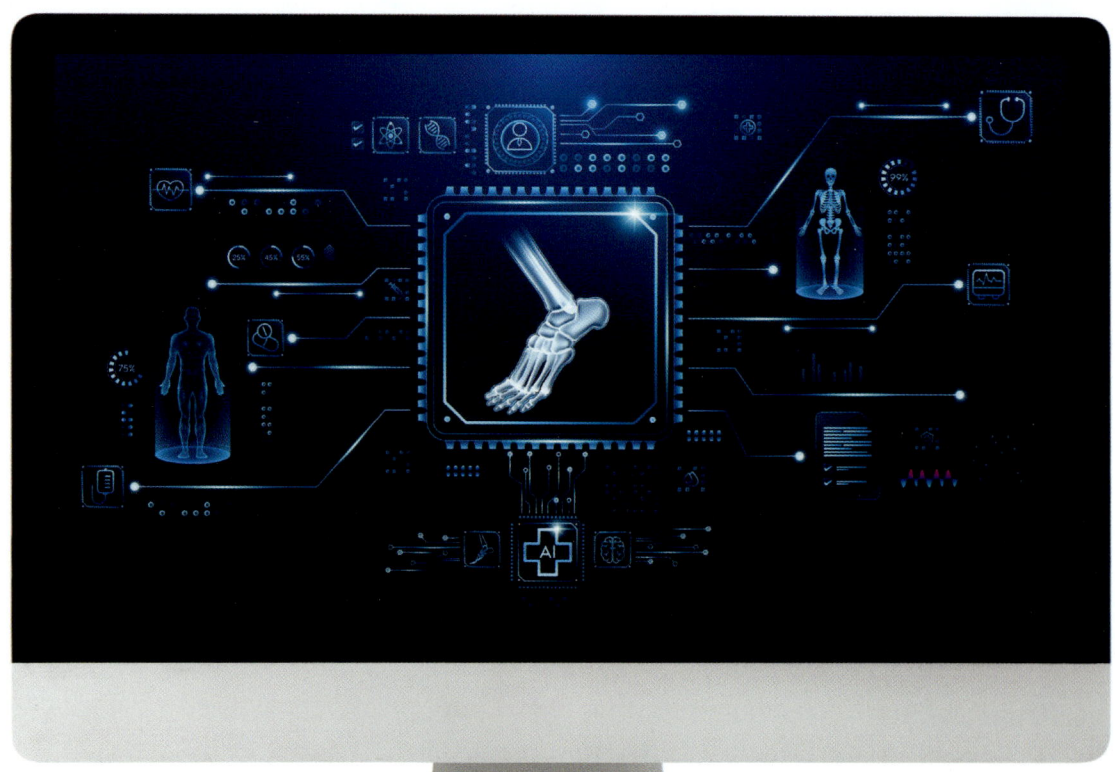

Someday, a chatbot might diagnose a patient all by itself. AI might decide how best to treat an illness.

CHAPTER 3   17

Scientists are using AI to match patients to the best medicines. AI looks at a lot of information. It looks at a person's **genes**. It looks at test results. It looks at symptoms. Based on it all, AI suggests the best medicine for that patient.

CHAPTER 3

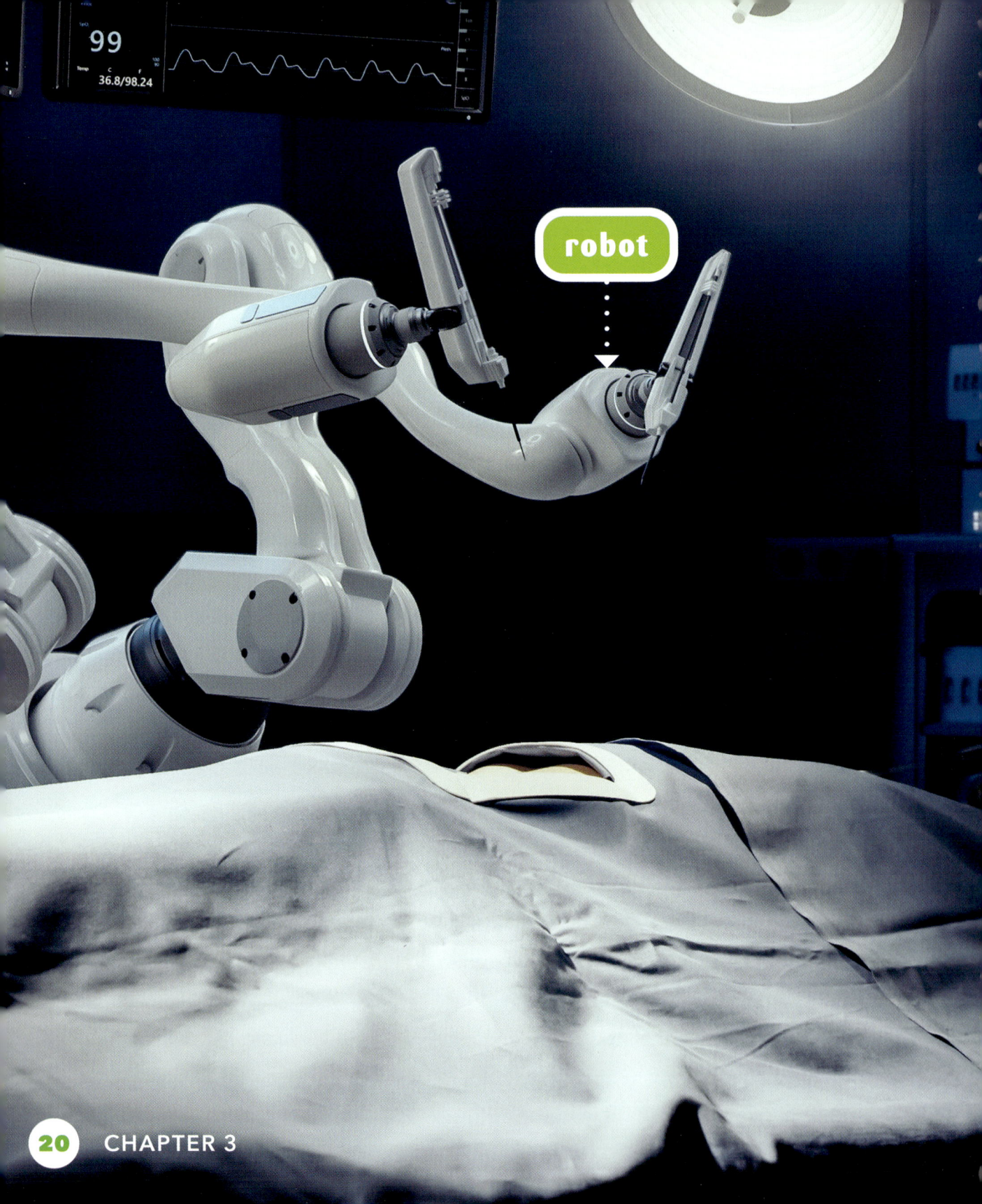

Some robots are trained to **operate**. Doctors are in control. But robots help. They are learning to do more on their own with AI. Maybe one day you will meet a robot doctor!

DID YOU KNOW?

By 2020, 90 percent of hospitals had plans to use AI.

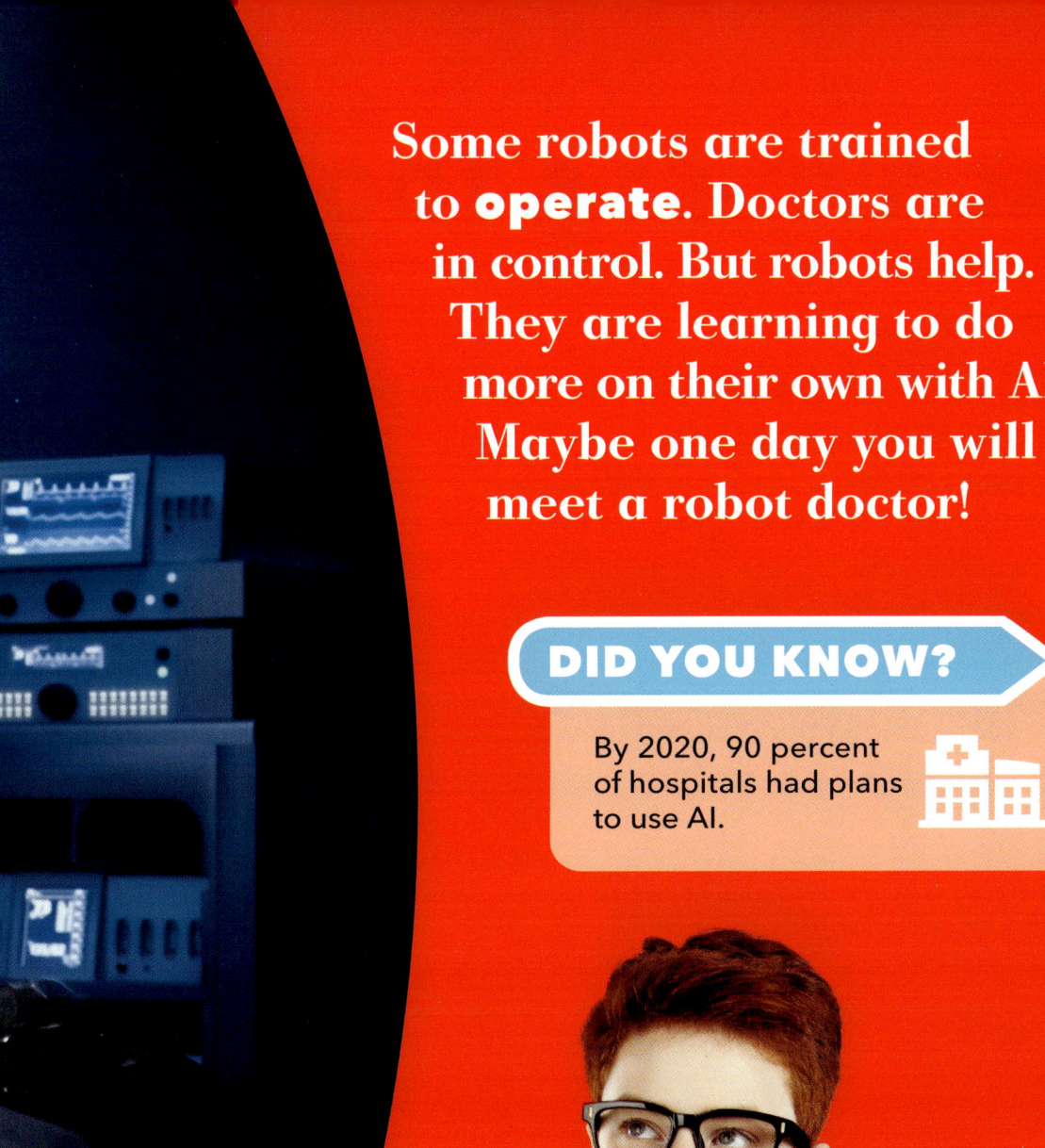

CHAPTER 3

ACTIVITIES & TOOLS

TRY THIS!

MAKE NEW MEDICAL AI

What could AI do for your doctor? Come up with some new ideas with this fun activity!

What You Need:
- paper and pencil or a device for taking notes

1. Think about the last time you went to the doctor's office. List all the things that happened.

2. How could AI have helped the nurse or doctor? Write down your ideas.

3. Could AI have helped you? What could AI have done to make the visit go more smoothly? Write down your ideas. Share them with a friend or family member.

GLOSSARY

artificial intelligence: The science of making computers do things that previously needed human intelligence, such as understanding language.

cancer: A serious disease in which some cells in the body grow faster than normal cells and destroy healthy organs and tissues.

chatbots: Computer programs that communicate with people.

diagnose: To determine what disease a patient has or what the cause of a problem is.

genes: Parts of DNA that have information needed to make parts of the body.

medicines: Substances that are used to treat illnesses.

MRI: A procedure that takes computerized images of the inside of a person's body.

operate: To repair or remove something from a person's body.

patients: People who receive treatment from a doctor.

robot: A machine that is programmed to perform complex human tasks.

summary: A brief statement that gives the main points or ideas of something that has been said or written.

swabs: Uses a Q-tip to take a small amount of something in order to test it.

symptoms: Signs of an illness.

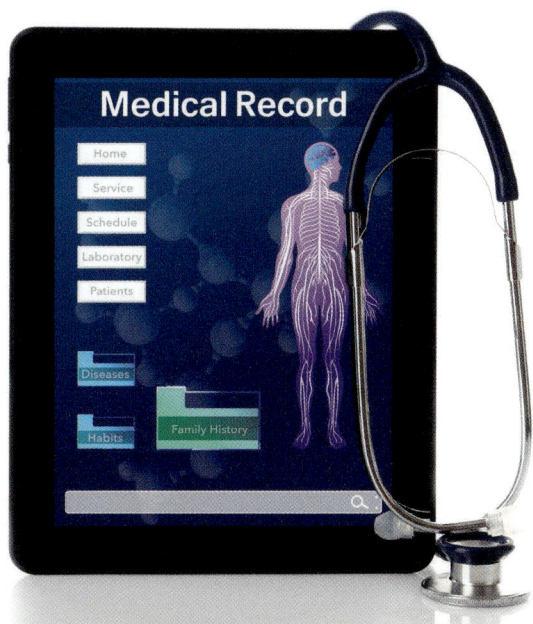

INDEX

chatbots 10, 11, 17
check 8
computers 5, 8, 13
diagnose 13, 17
doctor 4, 5, 6, 8, 10, 11, 13, 21
DXplain 13
genes 18
language 5
medicines 7, 14, 16, 18
MRI images 13

notes 6, 8
operate 21
patients 6, 8, 10, 11, 13, 17, 18
questions 10, 11
record 7
robot 4, 5, 21
sick 4, 10, 11
summary 8
symptoms 8, 11, 13, 18
test results 7, 18

TO LEARN MORE

Finding more information is as easy as 1, 2, 3.
1. Go to www.factsurfer.com
2. Enter "AIinmedicine" into the search box.
3. Choose your book to see a list of websites.